FORESTRY COMMISSION

Booklet No. 15

Know Your Conifers

by HERBERT L. EDLIN, B.SC.

Forestry Commission

LONDON: HER MAJESTY'S STATIONERY OFFICE

1970

First published January 1966

Second edition 1970   SBN 11 710006 4

Key to Cover Picture

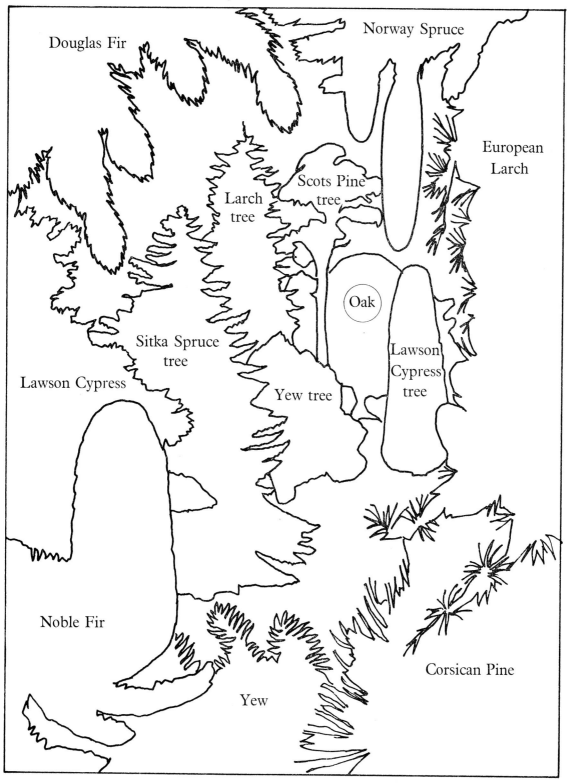

Douglas Fir

Norway Spruce

European Larch

Larch tree

Scots Pine tree

Oak

Sitka Spruce tree

Lawson Cypress tree

Lawson Cypress

Yew tree

Noble Fir

Corsican Pine

Yew

Contents

Introduction

Conifers, or softwood trees, form a distinct group which has become very important in the world's economy because they grow fast on poor soils even under harsh climates, and yield timbers that are very suitable for industry. They are now being planted and tended on a growing scale in most countries as a source of wealth, and this booklet shows you how to identify those commonly found in British woods.

By comparison with the broadleaved trees or hardwoods, the conifers have a simple structure and pattern of growth. Because they vary so little, one must look closely at their foliage before one can say which kind is which. Further, their names can be confusing unless one follows the simple rules that foresters, both in Britain and America, have adopted for the main groups called *genera;* or else the closely allied system of Latin scientific names, which is used internationally and also classifies trees by their genera.

First of all, you must make sure that the tree you are looking at is in fact a conifer, and not some unusual broadleaved tree. Distinctive characters of the conifers include:

(a) *Narrow, needle-like or scale-like leaves.*
(b) *Foliage usually evergreen (the only common exception being the larches).*
(c) *Scaly buds.*
(d) *Regular, almost geometrical, branching habit.*
(e) *Resinous fragrance of foliage, buds, bark and timber.*
(f) *Male and female flowers always borne separately, though usually on the same tree.*
(g) *Flowers always wind-pollinated, and therefore catkin-like, lacking showy petals or nectar.*
(h) *Fruit in the form of a woody cone (rarely, as in yew and juniper, a fleshy berry).*
(i) *Seeds usually winged.*
(j) *Seedlings of most kinds have numerous seed-leaves or cotyledons.*

Only one common broadleaved tree, the alder, has a fruit-body at all like a cone. But the alder is a deciduous tree with an irregular branching habit and curious stalked buds, so at no season of the year are you at all likely to mistake it for a conifer.

Botanically, the conifers are classed as Gymnosperms, or "naked seeded" plants, because their ovules, which later become seeds, are borne exposed on the scales of the imma-

ture cones or female flowers. These ovules are fertilised, as with other plants, by pollen carried from male flowers. As the cones develop, their scales become tightly shut to protect the seeds within. But when once they are ripe the cone-scales open in dry weather, and then the winged seeds drift away. Most conifers flower in spring; their cones may ripen during the following autumn, the following spring, or in some species eighteen months after pollination.

If the seeds alight on suitable ground, and are not eaten up by squirrels, mice, birds, or insects, they germinate and produce a little whorl of seed-leaves, only two or three for some species but numerous in others. These are followed by an upright shoot that bears solitary needles, forming what is called "juvenile" foliage. Such solitary needles are found at the tops or tips of most sorts of conifers, and as they all look much alike they give little help towards identification. But the shoots formed in the seedling's *second* year, and on side or secondary branches in the foliage generally, have an "adult" pattern of leaves. This is very distinctive for each genus of tree, and the following section shows how the genera can be sorted out with its aid.

In natural forests throughout the temperate zones of the world, and on mountain ranges in the tropics, conifers grow readily from seed, unaided by man. In cultivation they are raised in nurseries, nearly always from a seed, since most kinds are very hard to grow from cuttings. So our pictures illustrate two important nursery stages—the one-year-old *seedling* and the *transplant*, a tree that has been grown to a larger size after moving (lining-out) into a transplant bed. One object of these pictures is to show foresters a good type of seedling raised in one year, and a suitable young transplant, two or three years old in all, for planting out in the forest.

The timber of conifers is always called *softwood*, though in a few species it is quite hard. On the whole, however, it is softer and easier to work than the *hardwood* yielded by broadleaved trees. This explains its much greater demand and value for most everyday uses, even though selected hardwoods, in small quantities suited to special purposes such as furniture-making, may fetch higher prices. Today the great bulk of timber used in house building, fencing, packing cases and boxes of all kinds, and as railway sleepers, telegraph poles, or pitprops, is softwood. For paper-making, which uses about half of the output of wood in the main timber-growing countries, softwood is more suitable than hardwood because, amongst other features, its fibres are substantially longer. Softwood is also very suitable for the manufacture of most kinds of artificial board, an expanding industry that gives us wood chipboard, hardboard, and insulation board. At the present time about nine-tenths of all the timber used in Britain, whether in the unaltered state or made up into paper or manufactured board, comes from coniferous trees.

We have only three native conifers, the Scots pine, the yew, and the juniper, and only the first of these ranks as a timber-yielding tree. Foresters have therefore brought in a large number of other kinds from Europe, North and South America, and the temperate parts of Asia. Many of these are grown only for ornament, in parks, gardens, and pleasure grounds. Repeated trials over the past hundred years have shown that about a dozen of these *exotic* or introduced conifers are very suitable for timber production in the British Isles, and these kinds are now planted on a large scale. Only these twelve, together with the three native kinds, are featured here, as a very much longer book would be needed to describe all the ornamental sorts.

Except for the yew tree, which has its own family called the Taxaceae, all these conifers belong to one large botanical group, the pine family or Pinaceae. So the first helpful stage in classifying them is not their family, but their genus, and the fifteen kinds described here fall in 10 genera. Each of these has quite distinct features, and all can be told apart by foliage alone.

But do not rely on a single feature when naming your trees. Look at the pictures and the main text before reaching a decision. Often some simple but unmistakable detail, such as the three-pointed bracts found on the cones of Douglas fir, will clear up all doubts very quickly.

The next subdivision of trees is the species, which is shown by the second word in each scientific name, for example, the European larch is *Larix decidua*, while the Japanese larch is *Larix kaempferi*, though both belong to the same genus, *Larix* the larches.

The differences between species are quite small, and call for close observation of form and colour, as explained in the general text. But these small differences are very important to the forester, because one species may thrive where a very similar one fails. For example, Sitka spruce grows well under exposure to salt winds along the west coast, but Norway spruce will not thrive there. Nowadays foresters often study even finer differences within a single species, such as the *provenance*, or original homeland of a particular strain, but these precise distinctions are seldom obvious to the eye, and they are not dealt with here.

Because several botanists may have given Latin names and descriptions to the same tree at different times, and only one such name is now accepted, it is necessary to add, in the full citation of each specific name, the name or initials of the "authority" for it. For example the Scots pine is called *Pinus sylvestris* L., after the great Swedish botanist Linnaeus, who first called it that and published a full botanical description of it.

All this may sound complex at first, but with a specimen of the tree before you, and these pictures and text as a guide, you should soon be able to name most conifers planted on a large scale for their timber. Descriptions of rarer kinds must be sought in larger textbooks but it is worth noting that most of them, too, belong to the ten genera whose foliage features are described below.

Footnote for Foresters

Our sketches of one-year *seedlings* illustrate the amount of shoot and root growth that a good nurseryman should expect to get in one season.

Even more important, our sketches of *transplants* show, for each kind of tree, the desirable size, sturdiness, and balance of shoot and root growth that are most likely to prove successful for forest planting.

How to tell the Genera
by their Foliage: Key Drawings

Botanists have classified the conifers by *genera* which are, fortunately, very useful to foresters who wish to name any kind. For example, all the spruces belong to a genus with the Latin name of *Picea*. All our commonly grown genera show quite distinctive leaf, or needle, arrangements on their normal, or "adult", side branches. So, to discover the genus to which any conifer belongs, all you need do is to examine a side branch carefully, ignoring the youngest bit nearest to its tip.

Note, however, that the characteristic leaf patterns *cannot* be found on the upright leading shoots, nor on young seedlings, nor on many of the ornamental strains grown in gardens. Such branches often bear "juvenile" foliage with a different pattern.

Having selected your side branch, note whether the needles are set in an open arrangement, so that you can clearly see the twig that bears them, or whether they hug the twig so closely that neither it nor the buds can be seen. In the latter event, the foliage as a whole will resemble the flattish fronds of a fern, and the tree probably belongs to the genus *Chamaecyparis*, which includes **Lawson cypress,** or to the genus *Thuja*, which includes **Western red cedar.** Turn to pages 49 to 53 to see which.

All our other common conifers have needles which stand clear of the twigs. In the genus *Larix*, the **larches,** they are set in clusters of twenty to thirty, all springing from a little round woody knob, technically a "short-shoot". As the larches are deciduous and lose their leaves in winter, all you can find at that time of the year will be the woody knobs, but these too are quite distinctive. See pages 22 to 29. The remaining conifers have their needles in groups of two or three, or else set singly. The **junipers** of the genus *Juniperus* bear sharp-pointed needles in groups of three, set all round the stem. The common form is a small shrub with a resinous scent. See pages 54 to 58.

Next, the **pines** of the genus *Pinus*, which are very commonly planted. These have their needles grouped in two's, three's or five's. The three common kinds featured here all have their needles in *two's*, that is in pairs that spring from a basal sheath. See pages 10 to 21.

This leaves a group of conifers with isolated needles set singly. On all of these, the needles on side shoots appear to form two ranks, though they actually arise all around the twigs.

One genus is easily known because the needles are very variable in length, shorter ones being interspersed with longer ones. This is the **hemlock,** or Tsuga genus, described on pages 59 to 62.

Another genus, *Taxus*, the **yews,** can be told by the leafy character of the buds at the tip of the twigs (pages 54 to 58).

This leaves us with three common genera that need rather more examination. Look closely at the foot of each needle

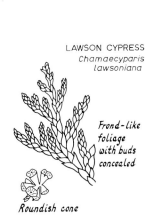

LAWSON CYPRESS
Chamaecyparis lawsoniana

Frond-like foliage with buds concealed

Roundish cone

Fern-like foliage with buds and twigs hidden; rounded cone: Lawson cypress.

WESTERN RED CEDAR
Thuja plicata

Frond-like foliage with buds concealed

Slender cone

Fern-like foliage with buds and twigs hidden; slender cone: Western red cedar.

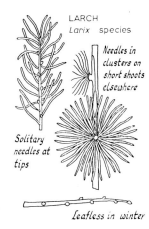

LARCH
Larix species

Needles in clusters on short shoots elsewhere

Solitary needles at tips

Leafless in winter

Needles in clusters on woody knobs: Larch.

to see whether it is springing directly from the flat surface of the twig, or whether it stands upon a little woody peg. If a peg is present, then the tree is a **spruce,** of the genus *Picea.* Check this by gently pulling a needle away; the peg will be drawn away also, leaving an irregular scar when it breaks off. Look further down the twig, to the point where older needles have *fallen* away; you will see that when the needles fall *naturally,* the pegs are always left behind, standing out like tiny hat-pegs. See pages 30 to 38.

If no pegs can be seen, then check as before by pulling away a needle. If it leaves a small round scar, then the tree is either a **Silver fir** of the genus *Abies* or else a **Douglas fir** of the genus *Pseudotsuga.* Check by looking at an older twig from which needles have fallen, and you will find that its surface is smooth, without projections.

The Douglas fir can easily be told apart from the commonly grown Silver firs by its slender, brown papery buds. The buds of the Silver firs are blunter, and often resinous. The Douglas fir is described on pages 38 to 42, and the Silver firs on pages 43 to 48.

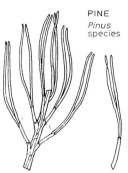

PINE
Pinus
species

Needles in two's, three's or five's according to species

Needles in pairs (as here), threes, or fives, with a sheath at the base: Pine.

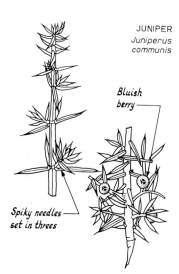

JUNIPER
*Juniperus
communis*

*Bluish
berry*

*Spiky needles
set in threes*

Needles in three's, all round stem, blue berries: Juniper.

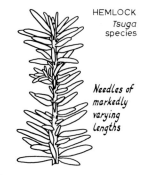

HEMLOCK
Tsuga
species

*Needles of
markedly
varying
lengths*

Solitary needles, irregular in length: Hemlock.

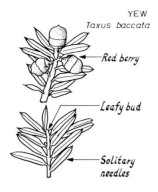

YEW
Taxus baccata

Red berry

Leafy bud

Solitary
needles

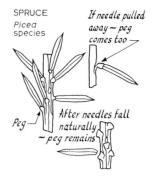

SPRUCE
Picea
species

If needle pulled
away ~ peg
comes too ~

Peg

After needles fall
naturally
~ peg remains

Leafy bud; red berries: Yew.

Needles on pegs: Spruce.

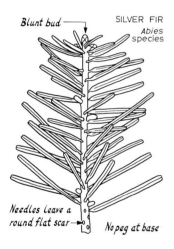

Blunt bud

SILVER FIR
Abies
species

Needles leave a
round flat scar

No peg at base

Needle arising from a flat, round base;
blunt bud: Silver fir.

Needle arising from a flat, round base;
papery, pointed bud: Douglas fir.

Oval brown
papery bud

DOUGLAS FIR
Pseudotsuga
species

No peg at
base

Needles leave round
scars when pulled off

Scots Pine

Pinus sylvestris Linnaeus

The Scots pine, our only native timber-producing conifer, is now found in its wild state only in Scotland and—very locally—northern England. But it has been planted everywhere and it grows readily from self-sown seed on heaths in many southern counties. It can at once be recognised as a pine because, except on the youngest seedlings, all its needles are set in pairs (see sketch, page 8). You can tell it apart from our other common pines by the colour and length of these needles; they are blue-green and relatively short—about 1½ inches long. Another key feature is the bark; Scots pine is the only common tree to develop a distinctively orange-red coloration (cover picture). As each portion of the trunk branches reaches an age of about ten years, the grey outer bark falls away and this striking red shade is exposed. On old trunks the bark, now pinkish grey, is often divided up by irregular cracks into broad flat plates.

Male flowers, illustrated on page 11, consist of clusters of golden anthers, set some way back from the tips of the twigs; they shed clouds of pollen in May, and then wither. The female flowers appear at the same time, at the very tip of a newly expanded shoot; they are tiny, crimson tinted globes. After fertilisation, they grow slowly during the next year into brown structures no larger than a pea; they need two years for full ripening. Mature cones (Plate 2), which are always "one whorl back" from the tip of the shoot, owing to its continued growth, are at first green with tightly-shut scales. When seed is needed, they are gathered in this state during the winter. Their symmetrical, "pointed-cone" shape helps the tree's identification; each scale bears a knob, but no points. In spring they turn brown and the scales open, to release the winged seeds shown on page 64. As in all pines, the seed is lightly held in a curved "claw" at the base of the wing.

When the seed sprouts, the seed case is raised above ground on a long stalk; it soon falls off and exposes a whorl of about a dozen seed-leaves, which are visible at the base of the foliage in our seedling sketches. As the shoot develops, solitary needles are borne, during the first season only; Fig. 46 A, and Fig. 1. Our transplant picture shows a tree three years old; it is a "1+2" transplant that has spent one year in a seedbed and two years in a transplant bed after "lining out". All its early solitary needles have fallen, and only paired needles remain. This example shows a sturdy stem and a good "balance" between shoot growth and bushy fibrous roots.

Though the Scots pine can be grown nearly anywhere in the British Isles, it is most successful as a timber tree in the warmer and drier districts towards the south and east. Its timber has a distinct reddish heartwood surrounded by pale-brown sapwood; it is resinous, but not naturally durable. In addition to the home-grown supply, very large quantities are imported from northern Europe, and this material is known in the timber trade as "redwood" or "red deal". Scots pine timber can readily be treated with creosote or similar preservatives, and is then well suited to use out of doors as telegraph poles, railway sleepers, and fencing. Under the cover of a roof, it serves as a leading building timber being used for joists, rafters, and flooring; other uses include sheds, pit props, box making, wood wool, wallboard, and paper pulp.

The timber of pines can usually be told apart from that of other conifers by the *absence* of small knots between the main knot groups; this is because pines bear all their branches in simple whorls, usually one whorl a year, without small intermediate shoots.

Old Scots pine trees, but not young ones, can usually be picked out by their rugged, irregular upper branches, resembling in outline a broadleaved tree.

The natural range of the Scots pine includes all northern Europe, northern Asia, Spain and Asia Minor. Seed of native Scottish strains, from either the west or the east of Scotland according to local climate, is preferred for present-day planting in Britain. The Forestry Commission has within its care some remarkably fine expanses of the old native Caledonian pine forest, notably at Glen Affric (see back cover) and the Glen More Forest Park in Inverness-shire, and at Rannoch Forest in Perthshire. Younger plantations of impressive extent will be found at Thetford Chase in East Anglia, in the New Forest, and at Cannock Chase in Staffordshire.

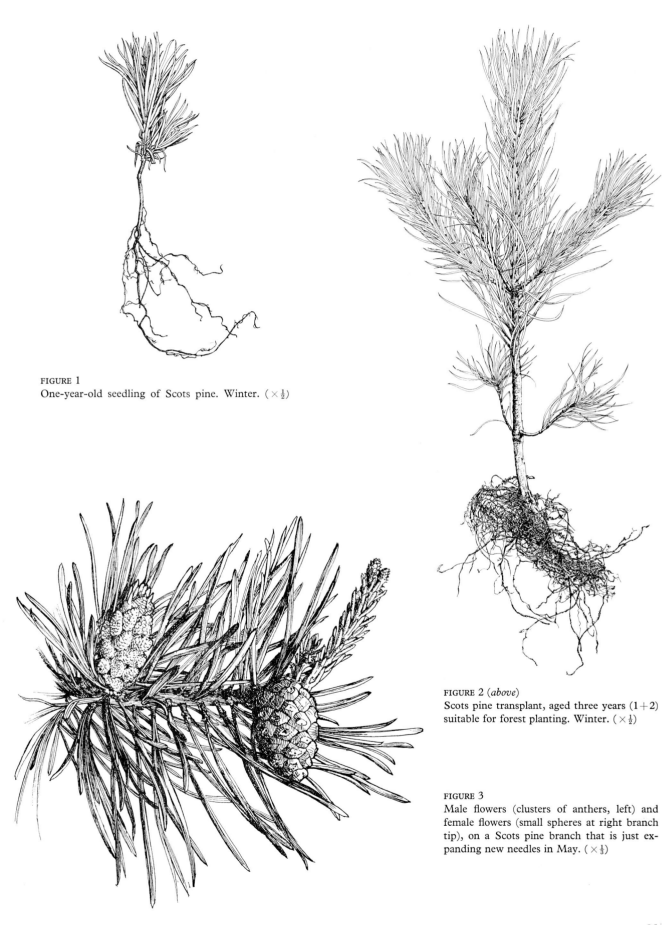

FIGURE 1
One-year-old seedling of Scots pine. Winter. ($\times\frac{1}{2}$)

FIGURE 2 (*above*)
Scots pine transplant, aged three years (1+2) suitable for forest planting. Winter. ($\times\frac{1}{2}$)

FIGURE 3
Male flowers (clusters of anthers, left) and female flowers (small spheres at right branch tip), on a Scots pine branch that is just expanding new needles in May. ($\times\frac{1}{3}$)

FIGURE 4
Scots pine foliage, with a one-year-old, unripe cone at the
branch tip, and a two-year-old, ripe cone, one whorl further
down. March. ($\times \frac{1}{3}$)

PLATE 1
Scots pines in winter, Castle Grant Estate, Morayshire, Scotland.
Aged 181 years; 83 feet tall; 81 inches in girth at breast height.

Corsican Pine

Pinus nigra Arnold variety **maritima** Melville

The Corsican pine is one of a number of local races of the Black pine, *Pinus nigra*, a tree with a wide distribution over the south and east of Europe. It has been selected for timber production in Britain because it grows fast and has a remarkably straight trunk, with light branches. Another local race, the Austrian pine, variety *austriaca* Asch. and Graeb., which has *straight* needles, was planted at one time but was found to grow too slowly and to produce too large and coarse branches; nowadays it is only used as a shelter-belt tree, especially along the coast, where it resists salt winds well.

The true Corsican pine is native only to the Mediterranean island of Corsica, where it reaches great size and age. It is only satisfactory as a timber crop in the south and the Midlands of England, the coastal fringe of South Wales, and along the east coast right up to the north of Scotland. These are all districts of low summer rainfall, with correspondingly high summer temperatures and duration of sunshine; in the wetter, cloudier districts of the north and west this Mediterranean tree does not really thrive. Our most extensive plantations are in East Anglia, especially at Thetford Chase and at Aldewood near Ipswich, but Corsican pine also grows well at Culbin Forest near Nairn on the Moray Firth.

Corsican pine is easily known by the length of its needles, commonly three inches long, by their distinctive *twist* which is well shown in our foliage sketch, and by their colour, which is a greyish-green or sage-green. Another key point is the shape of the terminal bud, which is broad at the base but narrows suddenly to a sharp point (Scots and Lodgepole pines bear long, blunt buds). The cones are larger than those of other common pines, shining mid-brown when ripe, and always one-sided or oblique in shape (cover picture). The seeds are about twice as big as those of Scots pine. The bark is grey or greyish-black to greyish-pink, but never red, and this explains the name of "black" pine; it is thick and fibrous, and is broken up by deep furrows on old trees.

Our pictures of a one-year-old seedling and a three-year-old (2+1) transplant show a feature that causes much concern to the forester. Corsican pine roots are remarkably long and slender, and hence they cannot readily take up enough moisture when the young trees are transplanted. For this reason foresters prefer to move young Corsican pine trees during the cold winter months, such as February, when the ground is moist and water loss from transpiration is low. Once established, Corsican pine can withstand severe drought, as is shown by its success on dry sandy soils in regions of low rainfall.

The timber resembles that of Scots pine, but where the two are grown under similar conditions the Corsican pine grows faster and forms wider annual rings; while in logs of comparable sizes the Corsican pine shows less heartwood. It is used for the same purposes as Scots pine.

FIGURE 5
One-year-old seedling of Corsican pine. Winter. (×2)

PLATE 2
Scots pine cones and foliage.

PLATE 3
Cones and foliage of Corsican pine.

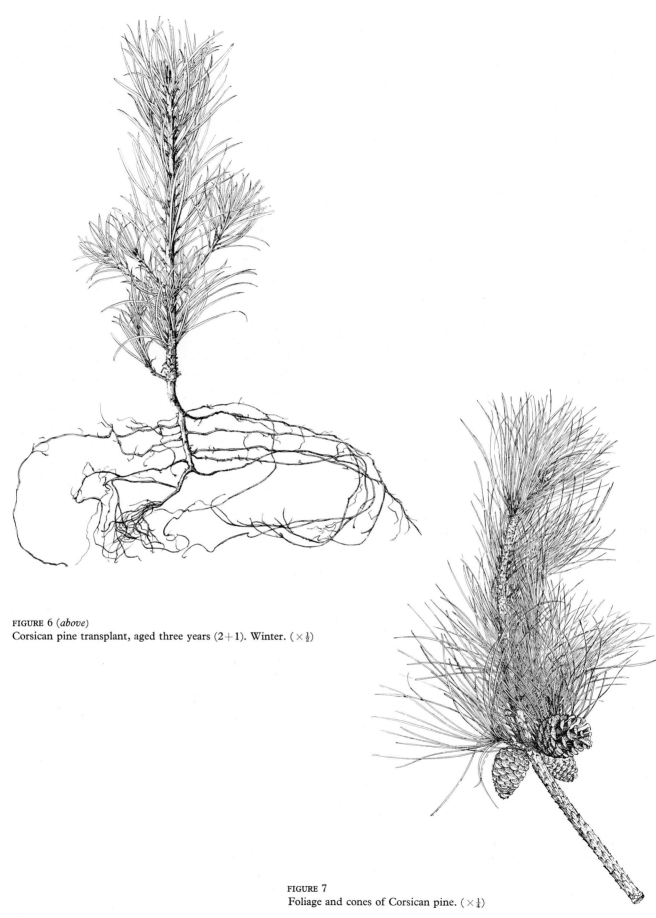

FIGURE 6 (*above*)
Corsican pine transplant, aged three years (2+1). Winter. ($\times\frac{1}{2}$)

FIGURE 7
Foliage and cones of Corsican pine. ($\times\frac{1}{4}$)

PLATE 4
Corsican pines, 100 years old, in the New Forest, Hampshire.

Lodgepole Pine

Pinus contorta Loudon

Many kinds of introduced pines have been grown on an experimental scale to see if they would thrive on poor soil in the west of Britain, where both the native Scots pine and the Corsican pine are unsatisfactory as timber crops. The one that has proved most useful, in Wales, western Scotland, north-west England, and also throughout Ireland, is the Lodgepole pine. As a wild tree this grows in western North America, from Alaska down to California, both along the coast and on the inland mountain ranges; it is important in practice to choose a provenance or local strain well suited to the climate where the plantations will be established. It is called Lodgepole pine because the Indians chose its straight stems to support their lodges or wigwams.

In appearance the foliage of Lodgepole pine is rather like that of Scots pine, but its needles have a mid-green tint, not a blue-green one. The bark is quite different to that of other pines; it never shows any red tint, but remains a dull brownish-black and it eventually breaks up into small, thin, squarish plates, divided by shallow furrows. The cone, as our pictures show, is somewhat egg-shaped, and each scale carries a small, sharp, prickle.

The foliage, as our pictures show, tends to be dense, with much overlapping of needles. The timber resembles that of Scots pine and has similar uses. Because of its remarkable tolerance of poor soils, including peaty moorlands, in our wetter and cloudier western districts, Lodgepole pine is now very widely planted there. Under comparable conditions it grows somewhat faster than does Scots pine.

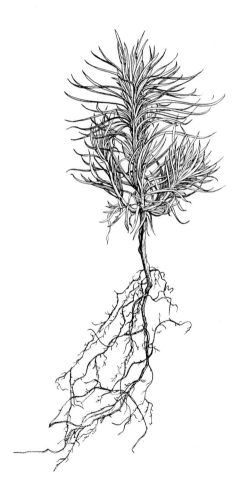

FIGURE 8
One-year-old seedling of Lodgepole pine. Winter. ($\times$1)

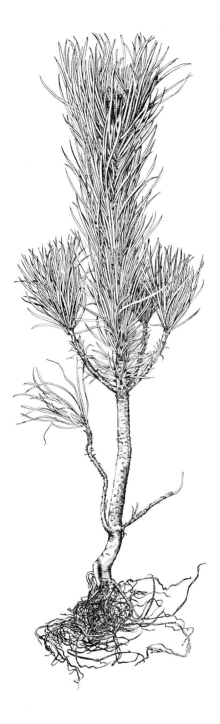

FIGURE 9 (*left*)
Lodgepole pine transplant aged three years (1+2). Winter. ($\times\frac{1}{2}$)

FIGURE 10 (*below*)
Cones and foliage of Lodgepole pine. Winter. ($\times\frac{1}{4}$)

PLATE 5
Lodgepole pines in Allerston Forest, Yorkshire.

PLATE 6
Lodgepole pine cones and foliage. Note the prickle on each scale.

European Larch

Larix decidua Miller

Larches differ from other common conifers in being deciduous. Each spring they put forth fresh foliage, at first a bright emerald green but becoming duller later. Each autumn their needles fade to a pale straw colour before they fall. But the needles on first-year seedlings, and at the tips only of other very young trees, are often *evergreen*, as our pictures show.

On larches of all ages, the needles at the tips of twigs, that is on shoots not over one year old, are always solitary. But everywhere else they grow in tufts or bunches, which are actually "short shoots" that never grow longer. The presence of these little knobs makes the larches easy to identify, both in summer and also when they are leafless in winter. The male flowers, borne in spring just as the delicate needles open, are clusters of golden anthers. The female flowers, often called "larch roses", are pretty flower-like clusters of scales, and may be green, white, or deep pink in colour. They ripen within one year to rather cylindrical cones (cover picture). These cones only slowly expand their scales, and when the forester wishes to extract larch seed he has to break them apart. The little seeds which eventually fall out and drift away are winged, the wing being firmly fixed to one side and lightly attached to the other.

The European larch, which is still the commonest kind though no longer that most frequently planted, can be told apart from other larches by its straw-coloured twigs, its true-green needles, and its straight cone-scales (Plates 8 and 9). It is native to the Alps and other mountain ranges of Central Europe, and has been cultivated in Britain since the seventeenth century. Because strains or provenances from high Alpine ranges are not well suited to the British climate, foresters prefer to get their seed from the Sudeten mountains of Poland and Czecho-Slovakia, where strains exist that are known to do well in the British Isles. Open-grown trees are shown in Plate 10.

Larch timber has a pale creamy-brown sapwood and a distinctly reddish-brown, or terra cotta coloured, heartwood. This heartwood is naturally durable, and though nowadays people can easily treat most softwoods—and also the sapwood of larch if necessary, to make them last just as long, this was formerly a great advantage. Larch timber as a whole has, moreover, better strength properties than most other conifers. For these reasons it is widely grown and used for fencing, gates, and estate repair work, and also in shipbuilding; the sturdy wooden fishing boats that are still built along the east coast of Scotland always have their outer planking made of a special grade of "boat-skin" larch. Larch is a very adaptable tree which grows quickly in youth, but each separate tree needs ample light and space, and so the total timber crop is rather light. It has often been grown in mixture with broadleaved trees, to help "nurse" or shelter them in their early stages. Sometimes you will find that a crop of larch has been thinned out and *underplanted* with conifers of another kind, which will take its place later on, and yield more timber; this is possible because it casts only a light shade.

Because larch starts growth so quickly, it is usually planted out when only two years old, and our transplant picture shows a "1+1" transplant. The bark on old trees is fibrous, broken up by shallow cracks or fissures.

FIGURE 11
European larch seedling, one-year-old. Winter. ($\times \frac{1}{2}$)

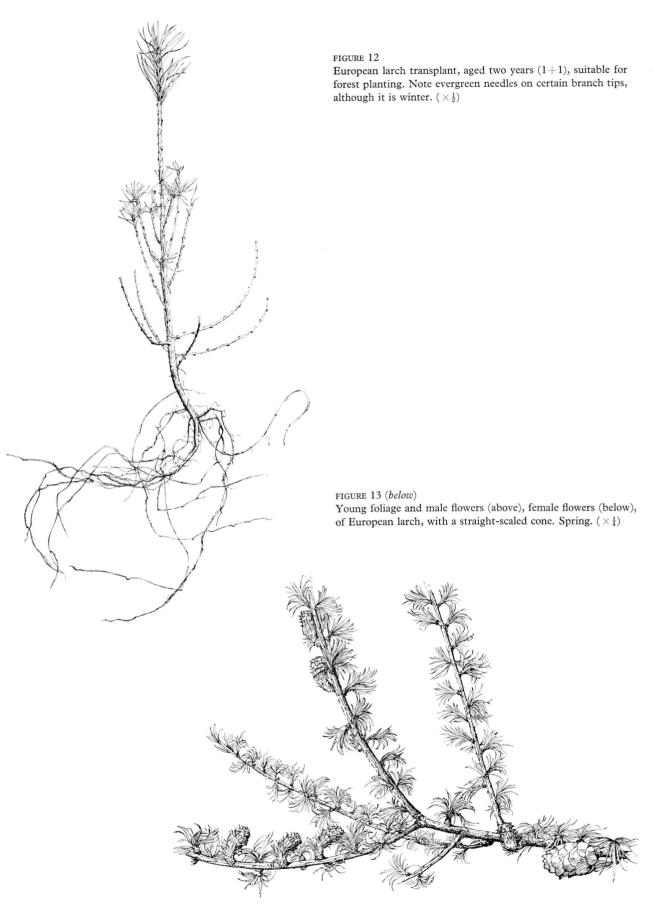

FIGURE 12
European larch transplant, aged two years (1+1), suitable for forest planting. Note evergreen needles on certain branch tips, although it is winter. ($\times \frac{1}{2}$)

FIGURE 13 (*below*)
Young foliage and male flowers (above), female flowers (below), of European larch, with a straight-scaled cone. Spring. ($\times \frac{1}{4}$)

PLATE 7
A European larch plantation at Hampden, Buckinghamshire.
Summer.

Japanese Larch and Hybrid Larch

Larix kaempferi Carrière and **Larix eurolepis** Henry

This tree, which grows wild on the mountains of Japan, was introduced to Britain in 1861, and began to attract attention as a plantation tree about 1910. Nowadays it is more widely planted than the European kind because it grows faster and seems better adapted to our variable climate. It is easily known by its russet or rust-red twigs, which look very striking during the winter months. Its needles are bluish green in summer, fading to orange in autumn. The cone scales are bent back or reflexed at the tip, so that each cone looks like a little rosette (Plate 8, Fig. 16).

The timber of Japanese larch is similar to that of the European kind, and recent tests have shown that it has comparable strength properties. This tree is often planted on old woodlands, particularly cleared coppices, where it is required to get a timber crop established quickly, ahead of the re-growth from the stumps of felled trees or cleared bushes. The transplant illustrated here is aged two years, or "1+1".

Hybrid larch, *Larix eurolepis* Henry, first arose through the chance cross-pollination of female flowers of Japanese larch by male flowers of the European kind. This happened on the estate of the Duke of Atholl, at Dunkeld in Perthshire, about 1904. Nowadays most of the seed for raising it comes from seed orchards set up by the Forestry Commission, in which selected parent trees of each kind are grown in alternate rows, to increase the probability of cross-fertilisation.

This "first-cross" shows to a remarkable degree the property called *hybrid vigour*. It grows faster than either parent, and will do reasonably well under poorer conditions of infertile soil or greater exposure than its parents can stand. It is not illustrated here because its characters are variable, but intermediate between those of the Japanese and the European kinds. A whole plantation can often be picked out from this circumstance, but it is less easy to be sure of any one individual tree.

FIGURE 14
Japanese larch seedling, one-year-old. Winter. ($\times \frac{1}{2}$)

25

PLATE 8
Japanese larch cone, above, has reflexed scales. European larch cone, below, has straight scales.

PLATE 9
Young and mature cones of European larch.

PLATE 10
European larches in a Shropshire park.

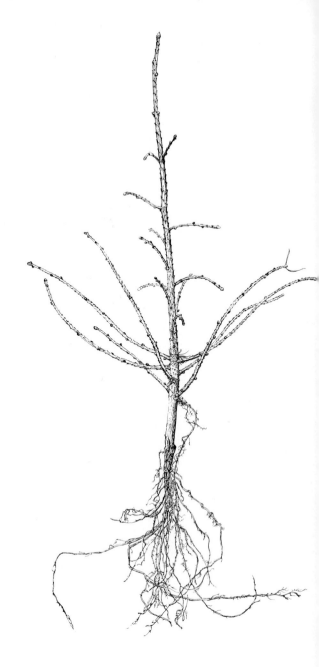

FIGURE 15
A sturdy two-year-old (1+1) Japanese larch transplant.
Winter. ($\times \frac{1}{2}$)

FIGURE 16 (*below*)
Foliage and cones of Japanese larch; note reflexed cone scales.
Summer. ($\times \frac{1}{4}$)

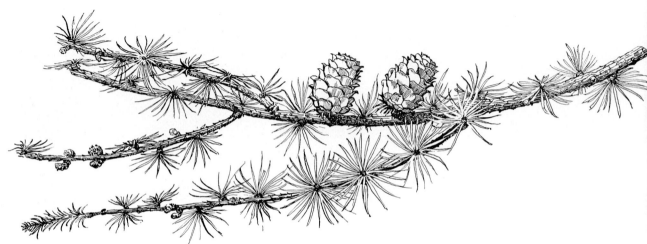

28

PLATE 11

Japanese larches in Coed Morgannwg, a Commission forest in Glamorgan.

Norway Spruce

Picea abies Karsten

Everybody knows the Norway spruce as the Christmas tree, used for winter decoration, but it is also one of the world's leading timber producers. It grows wild over most of northern and central Europe, and on mountain ranges further south, but it is not native to Britain. It was introduced at some unknown date, certainly by the mid-sixteenth century, and has been planted on a growing scale ever since. Though self-sown seedlings are sometimes found, nearly all our spruces are raised artificially from seed in nursery beds.

All the spruces are easily known because their needles stand on tiny pegs (see page 9). The Norway spruce is readily told apart from others by its soft mid-green needles, which are pointed but not sharply so. Spruce trees have a thin bark which appears smooth in general outline, not fibrous or furrowed, but has a roughish surface due to small irregularities. In the Norway spruce this bark, though greyish-brown in general colour, always has a reddish or rusty tint that aids identification; in fact the Germans call it the "red-spruce". The base of the trunk often spreads out in ridges or buttresses. The male flowers are clusters of yellow anthers, borne in May, which soon fall. The female flowers are greenish, oval structures that ripen rapidly, between spring and autumn, into very distinctive long, cylindrical brown cones, which have straight scales and always hang downwards (see cover picture).

The seeds that fall from these cones in spring are very small; each seed sits in a little cup at the base of its wing, to which it is only lightly attached. The resulting seedling is quite tiny also, rarely growing over three inches in its first year; so the forester leaves it for two years in the seedbed. It then spends one or two years more in a transplant bed before going to the forest. A good root system is needed because spruces are always planted with their roots spread out in a shallow fashion, just below the ground surface, beneath an overturned turf, or beneath the slice of turf turned over by a plough. Roots set more deeply would make no progress. Early growth is slow, but eventually the trees grow taller rapidly, and their stems bulk out fast, so that the total yield of timber is high.

The timbers of all the spruces are much alike and their properties are further described under "Sitka spruce", on page 35. Much Norway spruce timber is imported from Scandinavia and Russia under the trade name of "whitewood" or "white deal", and it is widely used in the building, box-making and joinery industries.

FIGURE 17
Norway spruce seedling, one-year-old. Winter. ($\times \frac{1}{2}$)

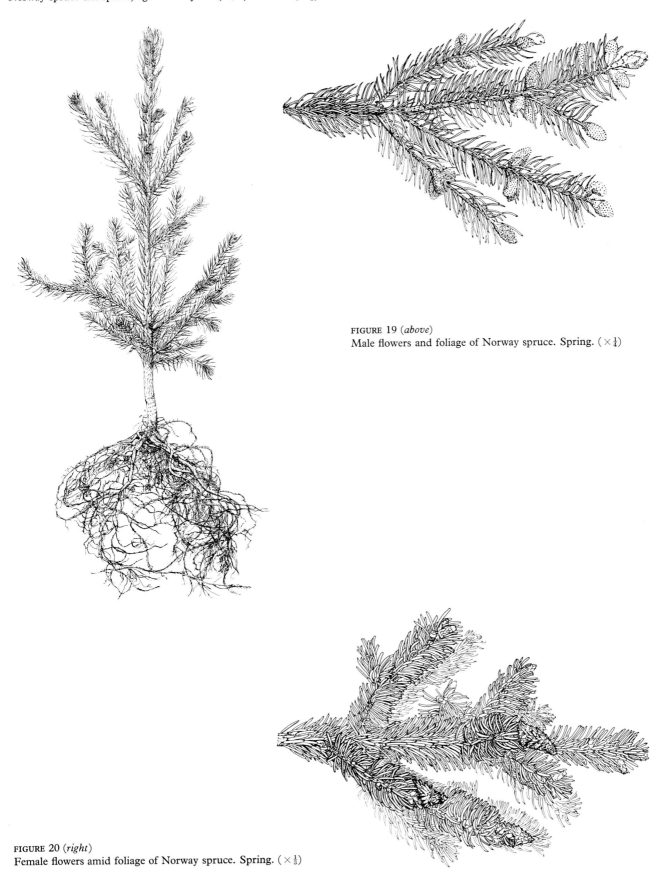

FIGURE 18
Norway spruce transplant, aged three years (2+1). Winter. ($\times\frac{1}{2}$)

FIGURE 19 (*above*)
Male flowers and foliage of Norway spruce. Spring. ($\times\frac{1}{4}$)

FIGURE 20 (*right*)
Female flowers amid foliage of Norway spruce. Spring. ($\times\frac{1}{3}$)

31

FIGURE 21
Norway spruce cone and foliage. Autumn. ($\times\frac{1}{3}$)

PLATE 12
Norway spruce in Kielder Forest, Northumberland.

PLATE 13
Norway spruce cones and foliage. In spruces, genus *Picea*, the cones always hang downwards.

PLATE 14
Noble fir cone. In the genus *Abies* or Silver Firs, the cones always stand upright.
See page 46.

Sitka Spruce

Picea sitchensis Carrière

Many spruces from Asia and America have been grown experimentally in Britain, as possible timber trees, but only one has proved a marked success. This is the Sitka spruce, named after the small seaport of Sitka in southern Alaska. Its natural range extends down the western seaboard of North America, from mid-Alaska to California. The seed needed for raising trees in the British Isles is often imported from British Columbia, Washington and Oregon as those strains grow vigorously in our climate. Sitka spruce is fairly easily known because all its needles have a bluish or slaty-grey tint. They end in a really sharp point, which makes the foliage rough to the touch, and rules it right out for use as a Christmas tree. The cones are very distinctive, being quite short and pale brown in colour; each of the thin scales has a crinkly edge, unlike that on other common conifers. The winged seeds are remarkably small, and the resulting seedlings are usually kept for two years in the seedbeds. The transplant illustrated is four years old, and has the good root system needed for shallow planting. Sitka spruce bark is thin and appears smooth to the eye, but is rough to the touch. It is greyish-brown in colour, and often breaks away in shallow plates. The base of the trunk is often buttressed.

For many years the Forestry Commission has planted more Sitka spruce than any other individual kind of tree. This is because it is well suited to the peaty hills and moors in Scotland, Wales and the north and the west of England where most poor grazing land has become available for afforestation. It enjoys a high rainfall, but in the south and east of Britain, where rainfall drops below forty inches a year, it is not really at home, so there it is seldom planted. On good ground in the west it starts growth slowly, but soon increases in height by as much as three feet a year. At the same time its girth grows rapidly, and as a rule it yields a greater volume of timber, in a given time, than any other tree. Further, it grows upright despite severe exposure, even to salt-laden winds blowing straight in from the sea.

The timber yielded so readily by Sitka spruce is very like that of the Norway spruce or "whitewood". As the name suggests, it is pale creamy brown, or almost white in colour. No colour difference can be seen between sapwood and heartwood, and only a slight one between the paler springwood and darker summerwood of each annual ring. It is even in texture, easily worked and holds nails well, and it is strong in relation to its size and weight. It has no natural durability out-of-doors, but the sapwood takes preservative and so it can be used for fencing or small telegraph poles. A good deal goes to the mines as pit props. Much is used for making boxes and packing cases, while there is an even greater demand in house-building, as joists, rafters and flooring. Selected material is used for joinery and ladder-making.

Spruce timber has proved very suitable for making various kinds of manufactured board, such as wood chipboard, insulation board, and hardboard, and much home-grown stuff goes to the board factories. The greatest world demand, however, now comes from the paper makers, who prefer spruce to all other timbers, no matter what process they use for making their paper pulp. It is also preferred by the makers of cellulose, cellophane and rayon fabrics. Much home-grown spruce wood now goes to newsprint mills at Ellesmere Port in Cheshire, or to the big semi-chemical paper mill recently opened at Fort William in west Scotland.

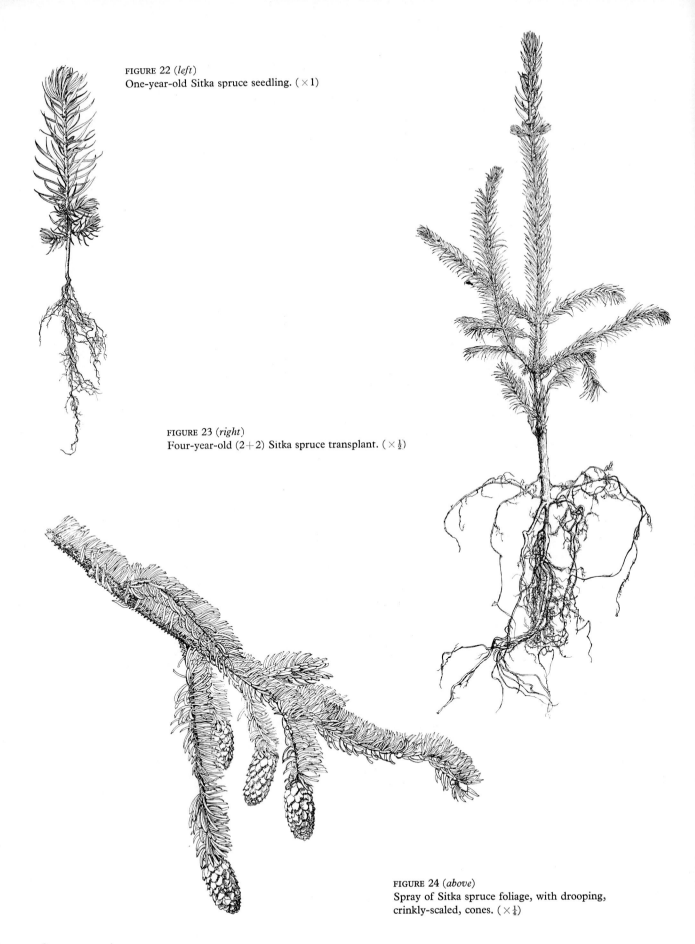

FIGURE 22 (*left*)
One-year-old Sitka spruce seedling. ($\times 1$)

FIGURE 23 (*right*)
Four-year-old (2+2) Sitka spruce transplant. ($\times \frac{1}{2}$)

FIGURE 24 (*above*)
Spray of Sitka spruce foliage, with drooping,
crinkly-scaled, cones. ($\times \frac{1}{4}$)

PLATE 15
Sitka spruce in Loch Ard Forest, Perthshire.

37

PLATE 16
Sitka spruce cones and foliage.

PLATE 17
Douglas fir cones and foliage. Note three-pointed bracts below
cone scales.

Douglas Fir

Pseudotsuga menziesii Franco

This beautiful conifer is named after David Douglas, the Scottish botanist who, in 1827, sent the first seed home to Britain. Its scientific name commemorates another Scottish botanist, Archibald Menzies, who discovered the tree in 1791. Its homeland extends down the western side of North America, from British Columbia to California; most of the seed we sow in Britain comes from the neighbourhood of Vancouver Island in British Columbia. There it forms magnificent forests, outgrowing other conifers and often reaching 250 feet in height. Here in Britain it has already become our tallest tree, with one specimen scaling 181 feet at Powis Castle near Welshpool in Montgomeryshire.

A few simple features enable you to identify the foliage of Douglas fir. The solitary needles do not stand on pegs, and if they are pulled away they leave a smooth round scar on the twig's surface. The buds are brown, scaly, and taper to a point; they resemble the buds of a beech tree, but are not so thin; these buds mark the Douglas fir out from the Silver firs, described later. The cone is very distinctive; it is egg-shaped and hangs downwards, and outside every scale there is a three-pointed bract such as is found on no other tree (cover picture). The bark is at first greyish-black and smooth, and bears resin blisters; later it becomes very thick and deeply fissured, and shows orange-brown tints in the cracks.

The male flowers of Douglas fir are clusters of yellow stamens which open in May and soon wither thereafter. The female flowers, borne near the branch tips, look like stout green shoots bearing leafy bracts; they ripen rapidly to brown cones, which start to drop their winged seeds during the following autumn. Seedlings grow rapidly and are occasionally transplanted when one year old. Our picture shows a three-year-old (2+1) transplant. Douglas fir is widely planted, but usually on the better ground, not in extreme exposure or on very poor soil. It is often used in the replanting of felled woodland; it stands light shade in youth so is sometimes given the protection of a light cover of birch trees. On good ground it grows fast, right from the start, and produces timber at a rate which rivals the spruces.

The timber of Douglas fir is marketed under that name in Canada and America, but when it is imported into Britain it is sold under the trade names of "Oregon pine" and "Columbian pine", probably because it bears a strong resemblance to true pine timbers. It has a well-marked reddish-brown heartwood that contrasts strongly with its pale creamy-brown sapwood. The annual rings are always clearly visible, for broad zones of dark brown summerwood alternate with the paler springwood. The timber works well and has good strength properties. It is used in building and general construction work, just as pine would be, and also in engineering as imported material is available in large sizes. Strong plywood is obtained from the big logs available in North America. Our home-grown trees are used for fencing, pit props, telegraph poles, sawmill timber, and paper pulp.

FIGURE 25
One-year-old seedling of Douglas fir. Winter. (×1)

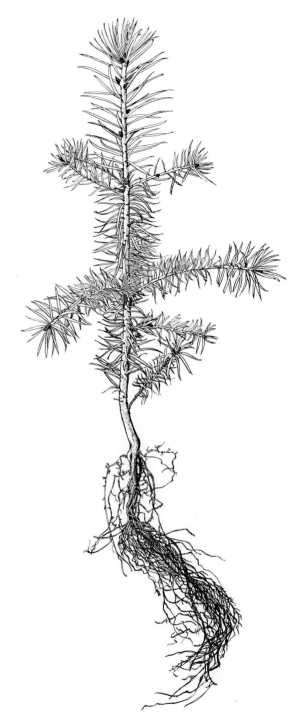

FIGURE 26
Douglas fir transplant aged three years (2+1). Note the slender
pointed buds. Winter. (×⅓)

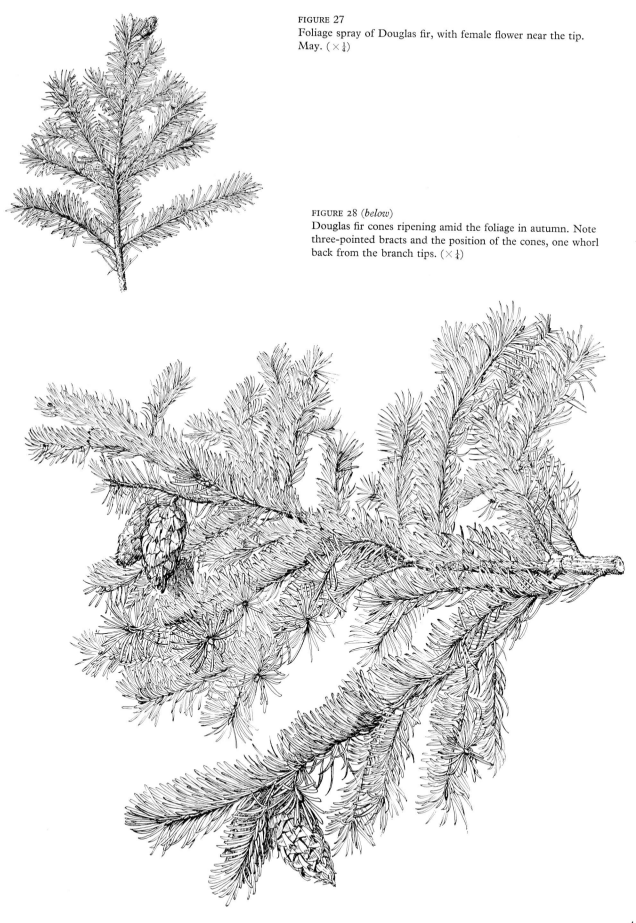

FIGURE 27
Foliage spray of Douglas fir, with female flower near the tip.
May. ($\times \frac{1}{4}$)

FIGURE 28 (*below*)
Douglas fir cones ripening amid the foliage in autumn. Note
three-pointed bracts and the position of the cones, one whorl
back from the branch tips. ($\times \frac{1}{4}$)

PLATE 18
Douglas firs in Parkhill Enclosure, Forest of Dean, Gloucester-
shire. Note figure at foot.

Grand Fir

Abies grandis Lindley

The Silver firs which make up the genus *Abies* are easily known by their needles, which are always solitary, and which leave a neat round scar on the twig when they are pulled away. A glance at the buds will distinguish them from two rather similar conifers; in the Douglas fir the buds are slender with brown papery scales, while in the yew the buds are small, with leafy scales free at the tips. No common Silver fir has buds quite like those; Silver fir buds are short, plump, and often resinous.

Silver firs always form erect stems and show a regular branching pattern. For many years their bark remains smooth, except for resin blisters, though old trees show shallow plates or fissures. The male flowers are like those of many other conifers, being simply clusters of yellow stamens, but the female flowers and cones are distinctive (see page 47). The female flower, an upright, green, oval structure which opens near the tips of side branches in May, expands rapidly during the summer, and is ripe by late August. Unlike other common cones, it remains upright, but only remains intact for a few weeks. Each scale has a bract below it, and once the cone turns brown both bract and scale break away and fall, releasing a pair of winged seeds. The central spike or axis of the cone remains standing for a year or so; it is called the "fir candle" and is a sure recognition sign. All this means that the forester who needs Silver fir seed must be quick off the mark, and collect his cones by climbing the tree as soon as they are ripe. It also means that intact cones are hard to store as specimens, even if held together by wires.

Silver fir seeds are rather large, and have a triangular wing firmly attached to both sides of the seed. They are hard to store, and in practice are sown in the spring after they ripen. The seedlings have few seed-leaves, three to six or so (Figs. 46E and 29), followed by normal foliage. They start growth slowly and are usually kept for two years in the seedbed; after transplanting they take another two years to reach the plantable size illustrated here.

People who have visited Central Europe will be familiar with the European Silver fir, *Abies alba* Miller, which flourishes on the Vosges, the Jura, the Alps and many other mountain ranges. During the nineteenth century this species was widely planted in the British Isles and some fine specimen trees still survive. Unfortunately, about the year 1900 a tiny insect, the aphid *Adelges nordmannianae* (Eckstein), which had been accidentally introduced from eastern Europe, began to damage the younger trees growing in Britain; it has proved so serious in our milder climate that the European species is no longer planted for timber.

In its place foresters use the Grand fir from western North America, which is shown here. Though it resembles the European kind closely, it suffers no serious harm from insect pests. Its needles lie in very flat planes, and are somewhat variable in length; its buds are resinous, a feature that distinguishes it from the European sort. Because it stands shade when young, it is often planted below birch, larch, or other trees giving only a light overhead cover. A

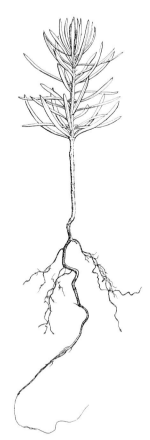

FIGURE 29
One-year-old seedling of Grand fir, *Abies grandis*. Winter. (×2)

43

good crop of Grand fir yields a great volume of timber in a relatively short time, and for this reason this tree is now being planted on a growing, though still small, scale.

The timber of the Silver firs is very like that of the spruces (page 35); in fact it is sometimes imported from Europe under the same trade name of "whitewood". It is pale cream or brown in colour, without apparent heartwood, and is suitable for joinery, house-building, box-making, and paper pulp; though not naturally durable out of doors, it is readily treated with preservatives.

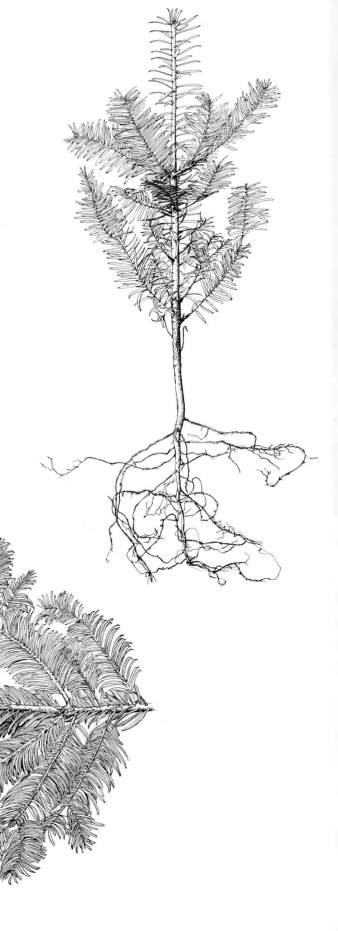

FIGURE 30 (*right*)
Grand fir transplant, aged three years (2+1); the buds are blunt. Winter. ($\times \frac{1}{3}$)

FIGURE 31 (*below*)
Spray of Grand fir foliage, with needles flatly disposed in two ranks. ($\times \frac{1}{4}$)

PLATE 19
Grand firs in Bedgebury Pinetum near Hawkhurst in Kent.

PLATE 20
Grand fir cone.

45

Noble Fir

Abies procera Rehder

This handsome conifer, which formerly bore the scientific name of *A. nobilis* Lindley, is readily known by the upswept form of the needles on its side twigs. These needles are a shining bluish-green in colour, and the whole tree is remarkably decorative; in Denmark it is preferred to all other conifers as a Christmas tree. Its native home, however, is among the western mountains of North America, where it grows to great size in vast forests. The growth habit is remarkably regular, but the trunk tends to taper more markedly than do most other trees; the bark is pale grey to purplish.

Noble fir cones are remarkable for their large bracts, which are bent downwards and give each cone a feathery outline; in America it is sometimes called "feathercone fir" (cover picture, Plate 14 and Fig. 36). In the west of Scotland the Noble fir has shown good resistance to gales off the sea, and also to harsh winters, and as it can give high yields of timber it is now being planted on a small scale in western districts generally. You are most likely to find it, however, as an ornamental tree. The timber resembles that of other Silver firs.

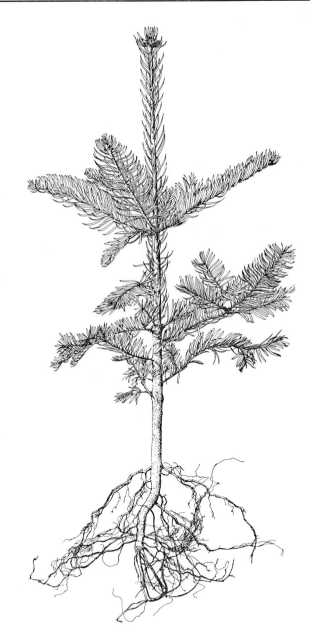

FIGURE 33 (*above*)
Transplant of Noble fir, aged three years (2+1); foliage is upswept. Winter. ($\times \frac{1}{3}$)

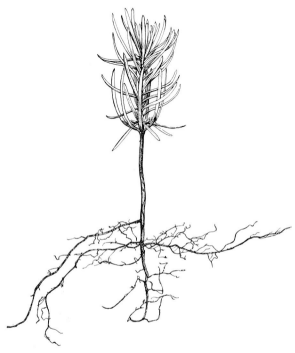

FIGURE 32 (*left*)
One-year-old seedling of Noble fir, *Abies procera*. Winter. ($\times 1$)

FIGURE 34 (*left*)
Female flower (centre) and foliage of Noble fir. Spring. ($\times\frac{1}{4}$)

FIGURE 35 (*above*)
Male flowers (centre) and foliage of Noble fir.
Spring. ($\times\frac{1}{4}$)

FIGURE 36
'Feathercone' of Noble fir; note reflexed bracts and also the
upswept foliage. September. ($\times\frac{1}{4}$)

47

PLATE 21
Noble firs in Bedgebury Pinetum, Kent.

Western Red Cedar

Thuja plicata D. Don, and

Lawson Cypress

Chamaecyparis lawsoniana Parlatore

These two trees are described together because they look so much alike that they are often confused, but only the *Thuja* is commonly planted for timber. Both come from western North America, and both have foliage that grows in flat plates or fronds, rather like those of a fern. The needles, though actually separate, hug the twigs so closely that they completely hide them, while the buds are also concealed.

One way to know the *Thuja* is by feeling the tips of the leafy twigs, which are smooth, stout and fleshy, whereas those of the cypress are thin and harsh. In colour, the *Thuja* is yellowish-green, with sometimes a hint of red, whereas the cypress tends to be bluish-greeen; but in an ornamental collection other colours will be seen. *Thuja* foliage has a peculiar fruity scent when crushed, while cypress smells more resinous. When the cones appear the two trees are easily distinguished. The *Thuja* has small, brown, slender cones each consisting of a few scales that separate close to their base. The cypress bears globular cones, each with a short stalk and a broad, rough-surfaced head; at first they are coloured cream, with bluish-grey knobs at the top of each scale, but when fully ripe they are blue-grey and brown (cover picture and Plates 22-23).

Lawson cypress is rarely planted for its timber, because it has no particular merits and one serious fault: its main stem is very apt to fork and this greatly reduces its value to the timber merchant. But it has become one of our most popular trees for garden hedges and ornamental planting; for it is hardy, evergreen, has a neat growth habit, and holds its foliage well down the stem. A large number of garden varieties are available, so nurserymen are able to say just how each specimen is likely to develop. Some sorts have blue foliage, others bright green, and still others yellow, and some are dwarf and others tall yet compact. Certain kinds have leaf and twig patterns quite unlike the type. All these rarities are increased by cuttings or grafting. The typical race, though not all the varieties, usually bears a drooping leading shoot.

Western red cedar, on the other hand, is usually grown from seed as a forest crop. In its seedling stage it is rather prone to suffer from the serious Keithia disease, caused by the fungus *Didymascella thujina* which can wipe out whole beds of young plants; but a fungicide has now been found which may check this. Foresters often use Western red cedar for planting below crops of other trees, such as larch or birch, that cast only a light shade. It grows fast when started off in this way and can yield heavy crops of timber. Several kinds of tree yield timbers known in commerce as "cedar"; this particular one provides the very durable and strong wood used for cedar bungalows, sheds, greenhouses, and roofing shingles; when first cut it is bright orange-brown, but it soon weathers to an attractive silvery grey. As the young stems are light, strong, and straight, they are often used for ladders, while because of its natural durability the Indians of western North America always chose this cedar for carving their totem poles.

The foliage of both Lawson cypress and Western red cedar is widely used by florists, for wreaths and displays, and when foresters prune away the side branches they are able to sell them at a profit. Both trees have thin, fibrous bark.

The tiny seeds that fall from Lawson cypress or Western red cedar cones are very much alike; each has a thin brown wing, about the same width as the actual seed, on both sides. When these seeds sprout, they first of all put out only *two* seed-leaves, which contrasts with the numerous seed-leaves found in other conifers. Then, during their first season of growth, the seedlings bear solitary needles around their first upright shoot, (See Figs. 37 and 46B). Whenever side shoots arise, and also when growth is resumed by the main shoot in the second year, the familiar fern-like pattern of foliage appears. But one has to remember that, when they bear only "juvenile" foliage in the seedbed, these trees look quite unlike their parents.

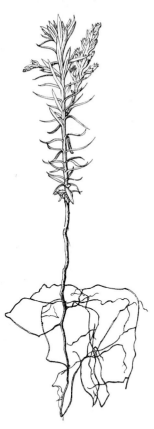

FIGURE 38
Transplant of Western red cedar,
aged three years (2+1); only
adult, fern-like foliage is now seen
Winter. ($\times \frac{1}{5}$)

FIGURE 37
One-year-old seedling of Western red cedar; showing solitary
juvenile needles on upright main shoot, and adult foliage on side
shoot. Winter. ($\times 1$)

PLATE 22
Round cones of Lawson cypress, before opening.

PLATE 23
Oval, tapering, unopened cones of Western red cedar.

FIGURE 39 (*above*)
Foliage spray of Western red cedar, showing slender
cones fully opened. Autumn. ($\times \frac{1}{2}$)

FIGURE 40
Foliage spray of Lawson cypress, showing
globular cones after opening. Autumn. ($\times \frac{1}{2}$)

51

PLATE 24
Western red cedars in Friston Forest, near Eastbourne, Sussex.

PLATE 25
An avenue of Lawson cypress and related species in Bedgebury
Pinetum, Kent.

Yew

Taxus baccata Linnaeus, and

Juniper

Juniperus communis Linnaeus

These two trees are included here because they are native, but they are never planted for timber. Each is easy to recognise and both, though classed as conifers, bear berry-like fruits.

The yew is easily known by its sombre appearance, with leaves that are dark green above, yellowish below; an isolated spray looks rather like a Silver fir, but the small buds have *leafy* scales. The bark is a typical rust-red, and breaks away in long flakes, while the trunk and branches are ribbed or fluted; this makes them of little value as timber. Yews flower in February or March, and the male flowers, which are tiny clusters of pale yellow stamens, usually appear on different trees from the female ones. The female flowers seldom attract attention, being small, oval, green structures set in the leaf axils. These ripen by October to the bright crimson berries, each holding a greenish-black seed within a cup, or aril, of pink flesh (cover picture). Birds eat the berries, and void the seeds; seedlings, each bearing two deciduous seed-leaves, spring up freely below trees where such birds roost. (See Fig. 46C).

Yews form natural woodlands on soils of many kinds, and are planted in gardens as hedges or ornamental specimens. Though animals rarely suffer harm from nibbling growing foliage, yew clippings are deadly poisonous to farm live-stock. The bark and the seed are poisonous too, but not the pink flesh of the berry. The timber is naturally durable, with a red-brown heartwood and a thin layer of white sapwood. It was formerly used for long-bows but now serves only for decorative furniture, turned bowls and ornaments. The association of yews with churchyards goes back to early Christian times, and some of these veterans are well over one thousand years old.

By contrast the juniper is a shrub, of very local distribution. You can find it on some of the chalk downs in southern England, and plentifully in certain Scottish Highland forests, but only in scattered patches elsewhere. You can easily recognise it by the peculiar scent of the sharp blue-green needles, which are always grouped in threes; this scent recalls that of gin, which is in fact flavoured with an oil distilled from juniper berries. Juniper bushes bear yellow male flowers and small green female flowers that ripen to fleshy berries, green at first but ripening by late autumn to purple globes with a silvery sheen. The birds scatter these, giving rise to tiny seedlings, each with two seed-leaves. Occasionally junipers assume a tall, narrowly conical, tree-like form, but they never yield really useful timber.

54

FIGURE 41
Spray of yew foliage, bearing berries. Autumn. ($\times \frac{1}{2}$)

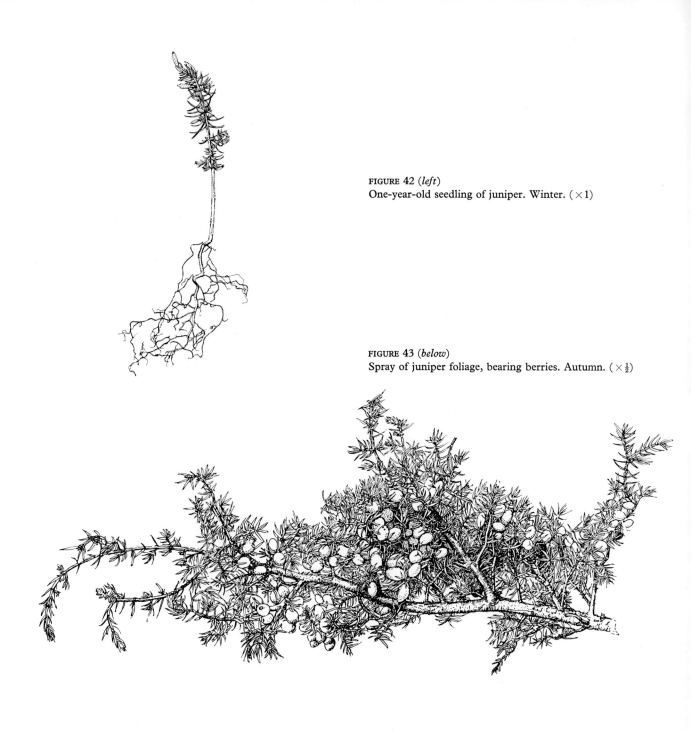

FIGURE 42 (*left*)
One-year-old seedling of juniper. Winter. (×1)

FIGURE 43 (*below*)
Spray of juniper foliage, bearing berries. Autumn. (×½)

PLATE 26 (*above*)
The famous yew in Selborne churchyard, Hampshire, 26 feet
round at 4½ feet above ground. This tree is featured in Gilbert
White's *Natural History of Selborne*.

PLATE 27 (*below*)
Juniper bushes on the Hampshire Downs, at Abbots Stone,
near Alresford.

PLATE 28
Berries and foliage of yew.

PLATE 29
Juniper berries and needles.

Western Hemlock

Tsuga heterophylla Sargent

This beautiful evergreen conifer owes its curious name to a supposed resemblance between the earthy smell of its crushed foliage and that of the hemlock plant, a tall, white-flowered poisonous perennial that grows beside rivers in southern England. Hemlock trees, however, come from North America and Asia, where several species are found, and this one grows along America's west coast, in British Columbia. It is now being extensively planted in Britain because it starts growth well in the light shade of other trees, and eventually yields a very heavy timber crop.

Among our commonly planted conifers, Western hemlock is easily recognised by an odd feature of its foliage: needles of various lengths are crowded together along the twigs in a random fashion. The seedling has three seed-leaves, an unusual number. (See Fig. 46D). It needs shading in the seedbed. Transplants grow in an oblique or sideways manner at first, but eventually the plant forms a straight stem with a characteristic *drooping* leading shoot. The small male flowers are yellow in colour, while the female flowers, borne on the same tree, are green. The brown, egg-shaped cones are very numerous, and look quite decorative on a specimen tree.

The timber, which is imported in large quantity from British Columbia, is pale brown, and is used for building, box-making, and paper pulp.

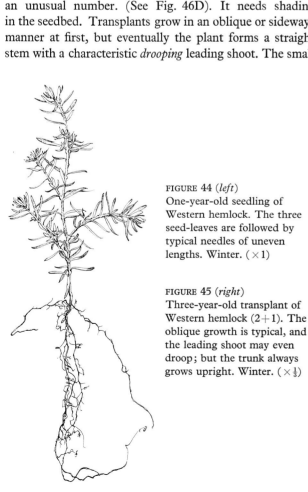

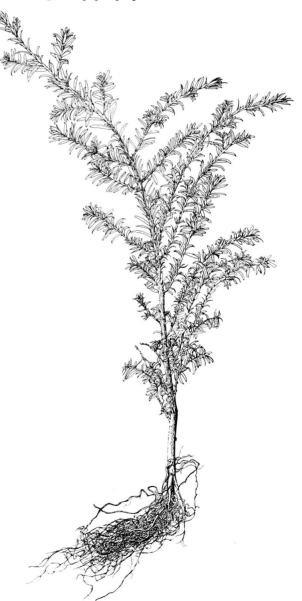

FIGURE 44 (*left*)
One-year-old seedling of Western hemlock. The three seed-leaves are followed by typical needles of uneven lengths. Winter. ($\times 1$)

FIGURE 45 (*right*)
Three-year-old transplant of Western hemlock (2+1). The oblique growth is typical, and the leading shoot may even droop; but the trunk always grows upright. Winter. ($\times \frac{1}{3}$)

PLATE 30
Hemlock cones and foliage. Note variable length of needles.

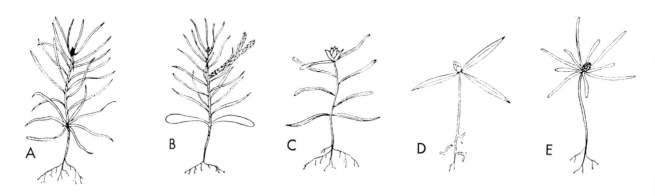

FIGURE 46
Early seedling stages of five conifers. A, Scots pine (p. 10), whorl of several seed-leaves, followed by solitary juvenile needles. B, Lawson cypress (p. 49), two seed-leaves, then solitary juvenile needles, with adult foliage on branch. C, Yew (p. 54), two seed-leaves, then normal foliage. D, Western hemlock (p. 59), three seed-leaves. E, Grand fir (p. 43), five long seed-leaves alternating with five true leaves or needles. Not to scale.

PLATE 31
Western hemlocks in Bedgebury Forest, Kent.

FIGURE 47
Foliage spray and cones of Western hemlock.
Autumn. ($\times \frac{2}{3}$)

62

Conifer Seeds

As shown in the drawings overleaf, the seeds of conifers show remarkable variations in size and form, which are of considerable scientific interest and may help people to tell the different kinds apart. Seeds are fairly easily obtained by shaking newly ripened cones, or by cutting such cones through the centre, lengthwise, with a stout penknife.

In most species the seeds are borne two per scale, though not every scale carries well-filled and useful seeds. Most kinds bear wings, which are always removed by the forester later on, for convenience when storing or sowing seed. Our drawings, reproduced at about twice natural size, show the seeds from various aspects. In the pines, for example, the front view of the seed—plus its wing—differs from the back view. In the cone, the seed always lies towards the central axis, with the wing outside it, immediately against the scale.

Pines have rather slender wings, which hold the oval seed in a little "claw", made of two slender prongs. Scots pine has seeds of intermediate size, Corsican pine larger ones, and Lodgepole pine very small ones. Larches have rather triangular wings and also triangular seeds which are very

firmly fixed to one side of the wing, less firmly on the other. Japanese larch seeds and wings are distinctly larger than those of the European kind.

In the spruces, the seed sits in a little cup at the base of the wing—and is lightly attached on one side only; Sitka spruce seeds are exceptionally small. In Douglas fir, the seed is firmly fixed to one side of the wing and lightly to the other, but the oval shape prevents any confusion with the larches. The Noble fir and the Grand fir are easily known by the large size and wedge shape of both wing and seed, the two parts being firmly fixed together on both sides. Western hemlock is also fixed on both sides, but the seed is very small and the wing is oval.

In Western red cedar we find quite another pattern; there are two wings, extending equally on both sides of the seed, each about the same width as the seed itself. Lawson cypress bears similar seeds. Yew seeds are wingless, and oval in outline; they are borne within a pink fleshy cup, which is not illustrated; there is only one seed in each berry. The juniper berries, drawn in full, hold several small, hard, wingless, triangular seeds, which are also shown.

CONIFER SEEDS

SCOTS PINE

CORSICAN
PINE

LODGEPOLE
PINE

EUROPEAN
LARCH

JAPANESE
LARCH

NORWAY
SPRUCE

SITKA
SPRUCE

DOUGLAS
FIR

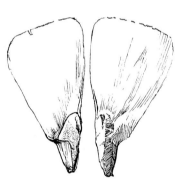

NOBLE
FIR

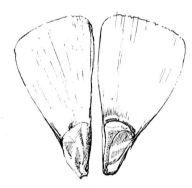

GRAND
FIR

WESTERN
HEMLOCK

WESTERN
RED CEDAR

YEW

JUNIPER

Printed in England for Her Majesty's Stationery Office
by Eyre and Spottiswoode Limited, Portsmouth

Dd. 153378 K.104